A GOOD DAY STARTS WITH KNOWLEDGE

This book belongs to :

____

____

____

Table of Contents

Introduction

Welcome to your calligraphy and hand lettering voyage!

We're delighted you chose us to help you embark on a fulfilling journey of discovering and mastering these two wonderful subjects. We know you'll enjoy the rewards of deepening your knowledge and getting to experiment with different tools, new writing surfaces, and basic techniques.

This book represents a starting point that helps beginners in the calligraphy and hand lettering arts develop their fine motor skills, memory retention, improve their mental health, and receive instant gratification having produced something by their hands.

This book is organized into two main parts: "Theory" and "Practice".

"Theory" has the purpose of explaining the main notions of calligraphy and lettering, as well as the different terms and tools that are used in these arts.

"Practice" is composed of two chapters:
1. "Calligraphy", where you will be learning how to write lowercase and uppercase letters, words, and some motivational phrases.

2. "Hand Lettering", where you will use the skills you acquired with calligraphy and put them into practice in an even more creative way, by also drawing symbols and different shapes and sizes of letters, part of some more motivational phrases.

We recommend that you don't rush through the book but rather take your time practicing the letters. Each letter/word/phrase is first written with a dark color to see how the end result should look. Then, there are several lighter shades of those letters/words/phrases so that you can use them as guidance and write over them. And finally, you have a lot of blank spaces where you can practice. If these spaces are not enough, you can experiment with other types of paper or mediums you have.

The only requirement is that you stay positive, open-minded, and give your best efforts. If treated with curiosity and intent, it will only benefit you in the long run.

We wish you a fantastic learning experience with these soothing arts! And remember, have fun with the book!

PART 1 - Theory

Calligraphy

vs.

vs.

Typography

There are many terms in the lettering world, which are sometimes used interchangeably, making it easy to create confusion between them. Knowing the differences between these terms will help you understand the area you enjoy best and search with ease the topics you want to study.

So, the basic lettering terms are the following:

Calligraphy: The art of writing letters by hand, with specific tools, like a dip pen with a nib and ink, using a variation in width for the upstrokes and downstrokes of each letter and varying degrees of pressure, all in a single stroke. Calligraphy is usually used in longer written pieces (like traditional letters) and involves basic strokes to form letters and words.

Types of Calligraphy

Traditional Calligraphy: beautiful handwriting using dip pens or fountain pens (the latter requires more skills, as most don't have a flexible nib, which is necessary to create thick and thin lines). Traditional calligraphy is defined by the contrast between thin and thick strokes within letters, which is achieved by correctly handling the tools used.

Brush Calligraphy: similar to traditional calligraphy, except for the tool used for writing. Brush calligraphy is done using brush pens or regular brushes for watercolors

Faux Calligraphy: it is useful for an introduction to the traditional calligraphy, as you can use any standard tool like a ballpoint pen, chalk, or marker. In faux calligraphy, you obtain the think and thick strokes by duplicating the downward strokes so that they look thicker than the upward strokes.

Hand Lettering: the art of drawing letters by hand, with each letter being sketched and drawn individually. With hand lettering, you usually have more control over the letters than with calligraphy. Hand lettering is used in projects that are too large for calligraphy, such as large chalkboards, headlines, logos, or short illustrated sentences. But you can also do hand-lettering on pieces of paper by using simple brush pens, pencils, or markers.

The *main difference between calligraphy and hand lettering* is that you can change the letter sizes and script types when hand lettering. In contrast, in calligraphy, the letters are in fixed-size relation to one another. In calligraphy, the words are written in one fluent motion and sticking to one script type, whereas with hand lettering, you often work with an under-drawing or sketch. Hand Lettering and Calligraphy are not defined by the tools you use but by the method you choose to construct the letters.

Typography: the art of designing and arranging the letters by using a digital program, which is then used in the printed materials or online. It might look similar to hand lettering, but the letters are grouped in a repeatable system (every letter looks the same).

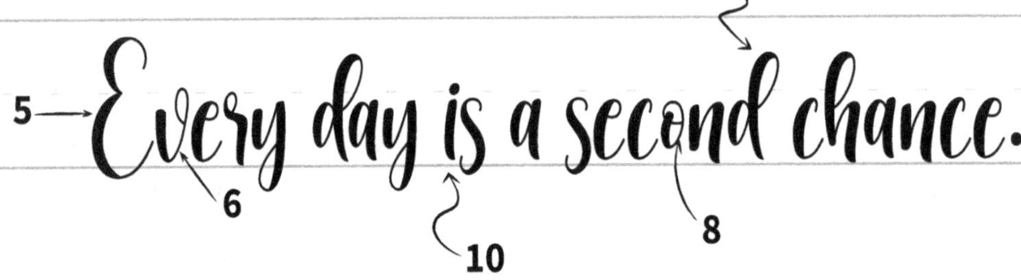

Every day is a second chance.

Stay hustling.

Take care of yourself.

Terminology

1. Majuscule – "capital" letter
2. Minuscule – "small" letter
3. Ascender – parts of the letters above the main writing line: "h", "l", "k", etc.
4. Descender – parts of the letters below the main writing line: "g", "y", "p", etc.
5. Downstroke – any movement downward with the writing instrument. The lines are thick.
6. Upstroke (or hairline stroke) – any movement upward with the writing instrument. The lines are thin.
7. Cross stroke – horizontal strokes on letters such as "t", "f".
8. Counter – the inside of a letter. It may be fully or partially enclosed: think of the difference between the space inside "o" and the space below "m".
9. Serif – small decorative strokes added to the end of a letter's main stroke.
10. Sans Serif – "sans" means "without" and refers to the letters that do not have a decorative stroke at the end of a letter's main stroke.
11. Baseline – the writing line on which the primary body of each letter sits.
12. Ascender line – marks the top of the ascenders.
13. X-height – the height of the minuscules without ascenders or descenders.
14. Waist line (or mean line) – the top of the x-height from the baseline.

Other terms you should understand:
- Weight – the thickness of a letter (downstrokes have a heavier weight than upstrokes).
- Stroke – any line made with the writing instrument.

Tools

When it comes to selecting the tools for calligraphy and hand lettering, the options are endless. The two fundamental tools are:

- **the writing surface**: paper, vellum, wall, mug, signpost, your wrist, etc
- **the writing instrument**: pencils, paintbrushes, brush pens, fountain pens, sharpies, etc.

Paper

Calligraphers usually use a smooth glazed paper. A smooth paper better reveals the broad-nib pen, and the strokes are more accurate.

For hand lettering, choose a smooth finish paper, like mixed-media or drawing paper for your final version of the project. But before that, you can use a cheap copy paper or tracing paper (preferably thin so that you can see guidelines through it) for practice.

Watercolor paper also works well with most pens and paintbrushes, and you can use it to add watercolor designs to your work.

Pens

There are various types of pens you can use with calligraphy and hand lettering. Some artists prefer using pens with fine point ink, while others choose thick brush pens. It's all about figuring out which pen works for your art. For starters, you can invest in a good set of fine tip pens. The small tips are perfect for little details, and the compact sizes excellent for filling in letters. Nevertheless, the most popular type of pens is brush pens. They are practically a different category on their own.

Brushes

A brush for writing has a lot of kinds and sub kinds. The differences depend on the material, size, purpose, and proportions. There are three main kinds of brushes: brushes of Siberian weasel, goatskin, and hare fur. A paintbrush with a round, pointed tip is ideal for watercolor calligraphy. Water brushes also work well. Choose a brush that springs back into shape after each stroke, so you don't have to keep reshaping the tip. This will help keep your letters consistent.

Pencils

For hand lettering, the essential tool you must have is a pencil. If you're just starting out, you can use just about any drawing pencil. Lead in pencils can either be soft or hard. Most calligraphers use a lighter pencil at first (these are pencils with harder lead) and then switch to a darker pencil (softer lead) once the design takes shape.

Your calligraphic and hand lettering life will be much easier if you also have:

- a **ruler,** ideally 50cm, transparent, and marked in cm and inches, which helps you keep your lettering straight or draw guidelines in pencil
- an **eraser** for correcting the mistakes. A great alternative to the conventional eraser is the kneaded eraser, which never leaves any particles or pieces after you erase it, and it will also never leave any smudges.
- **ink, watercolor, or artists' gouache paint**
- fine artists' **markers**, for ornament and decoration.

PART 2 – Practice

Calligraphy Practice

Style 1

Letters

PRACTICE WRITING THE UPPERCASE AND LOWERCASE LETTERS.

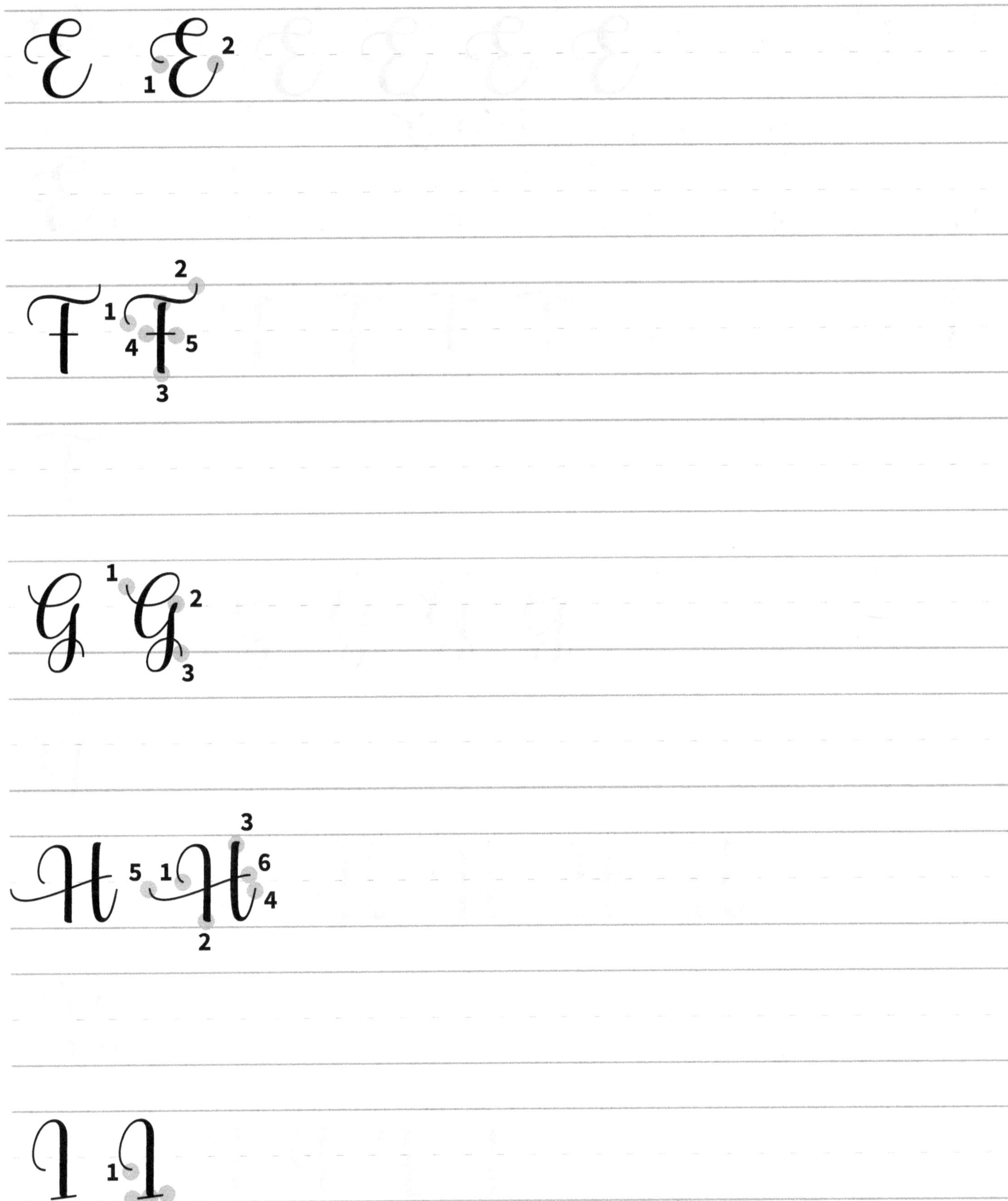

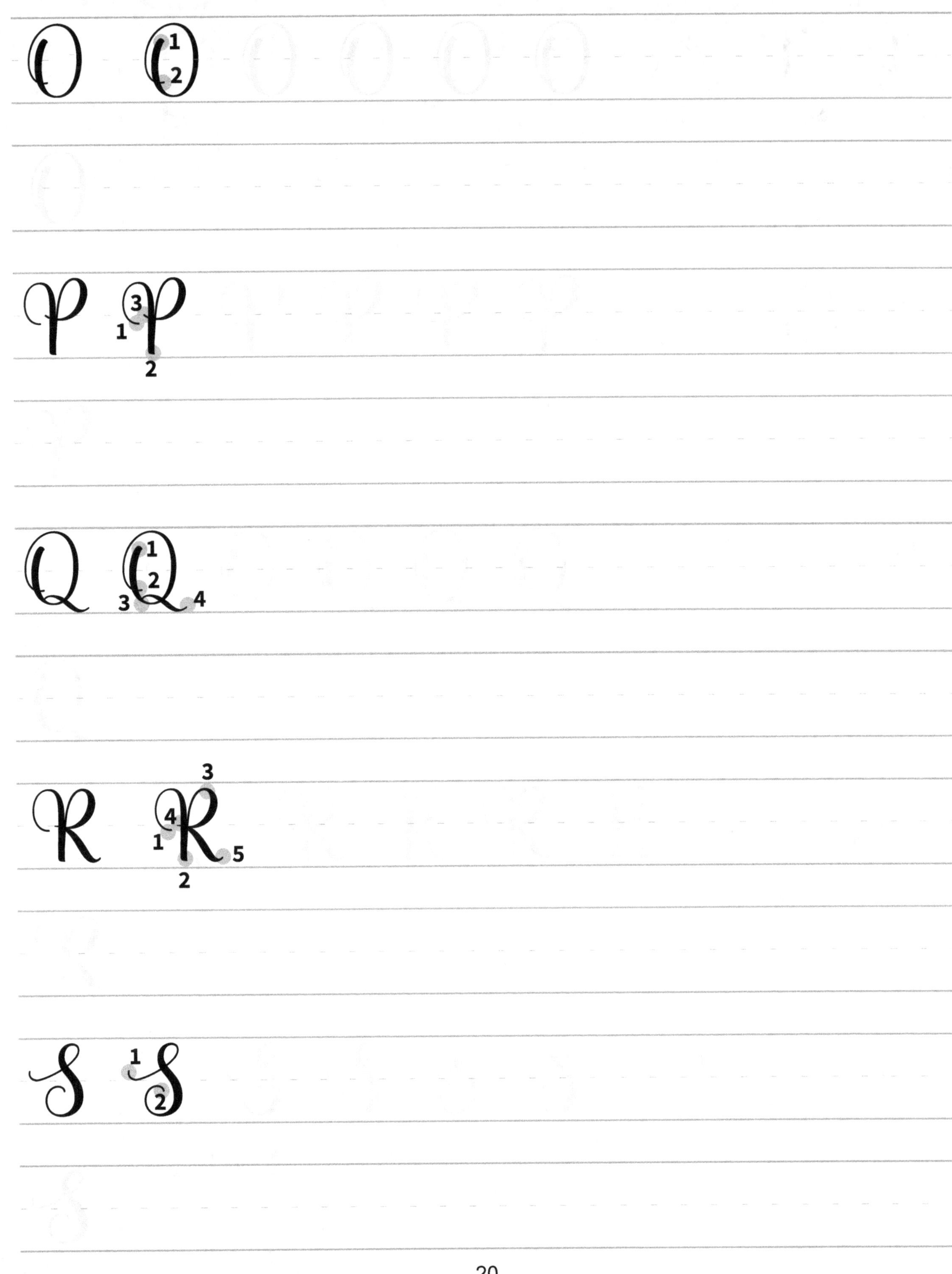

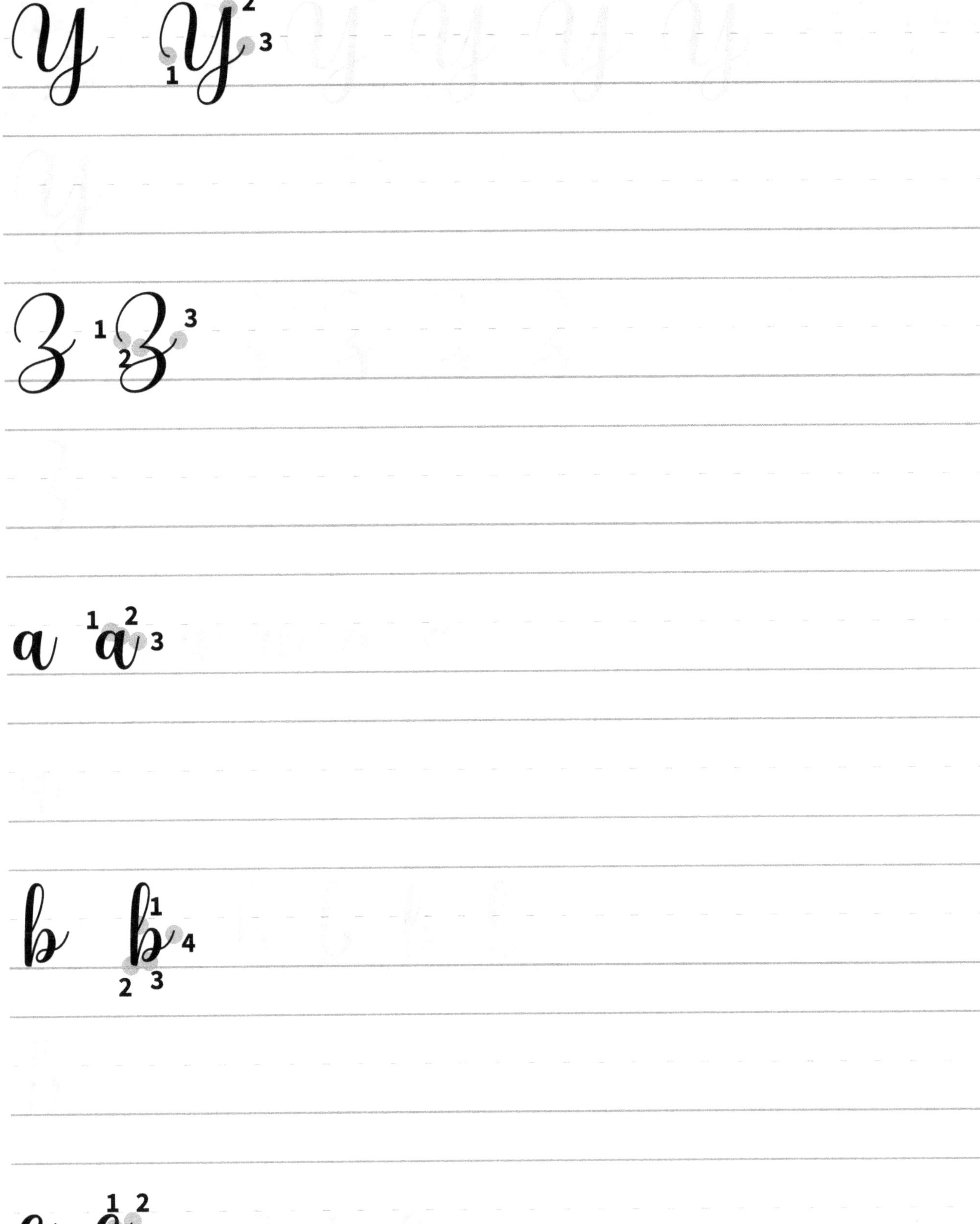

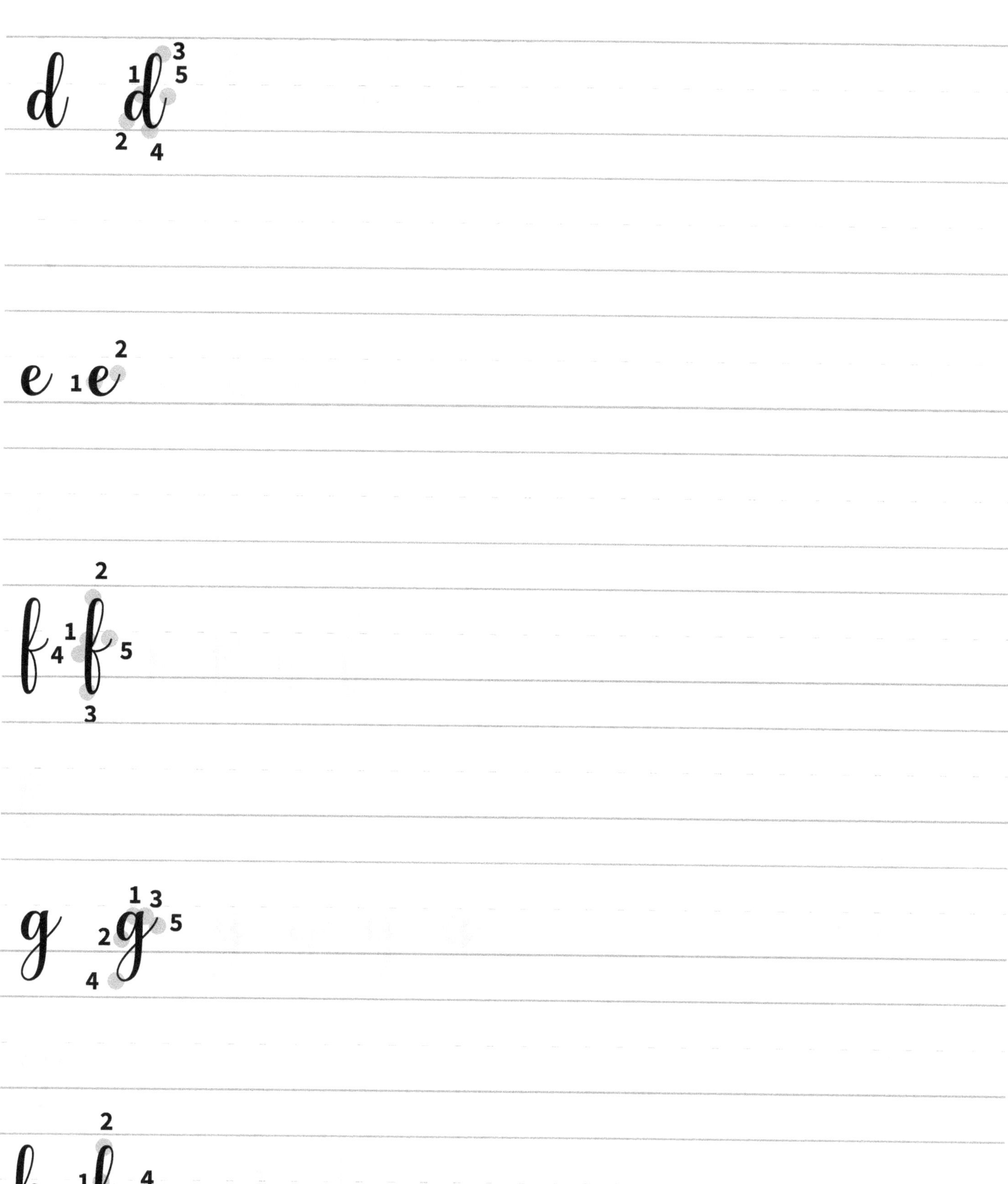

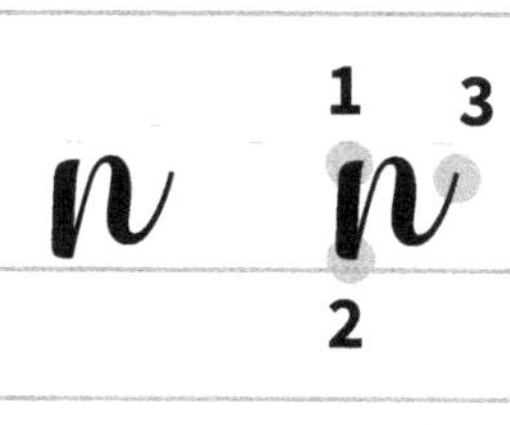

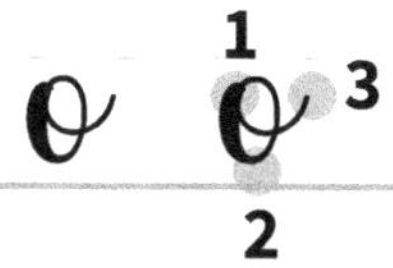

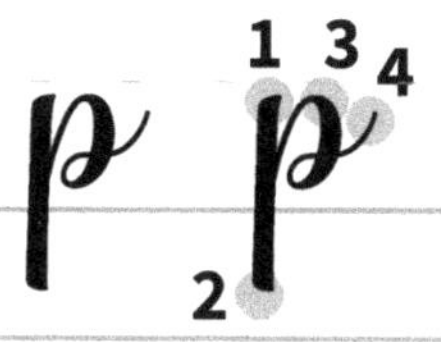

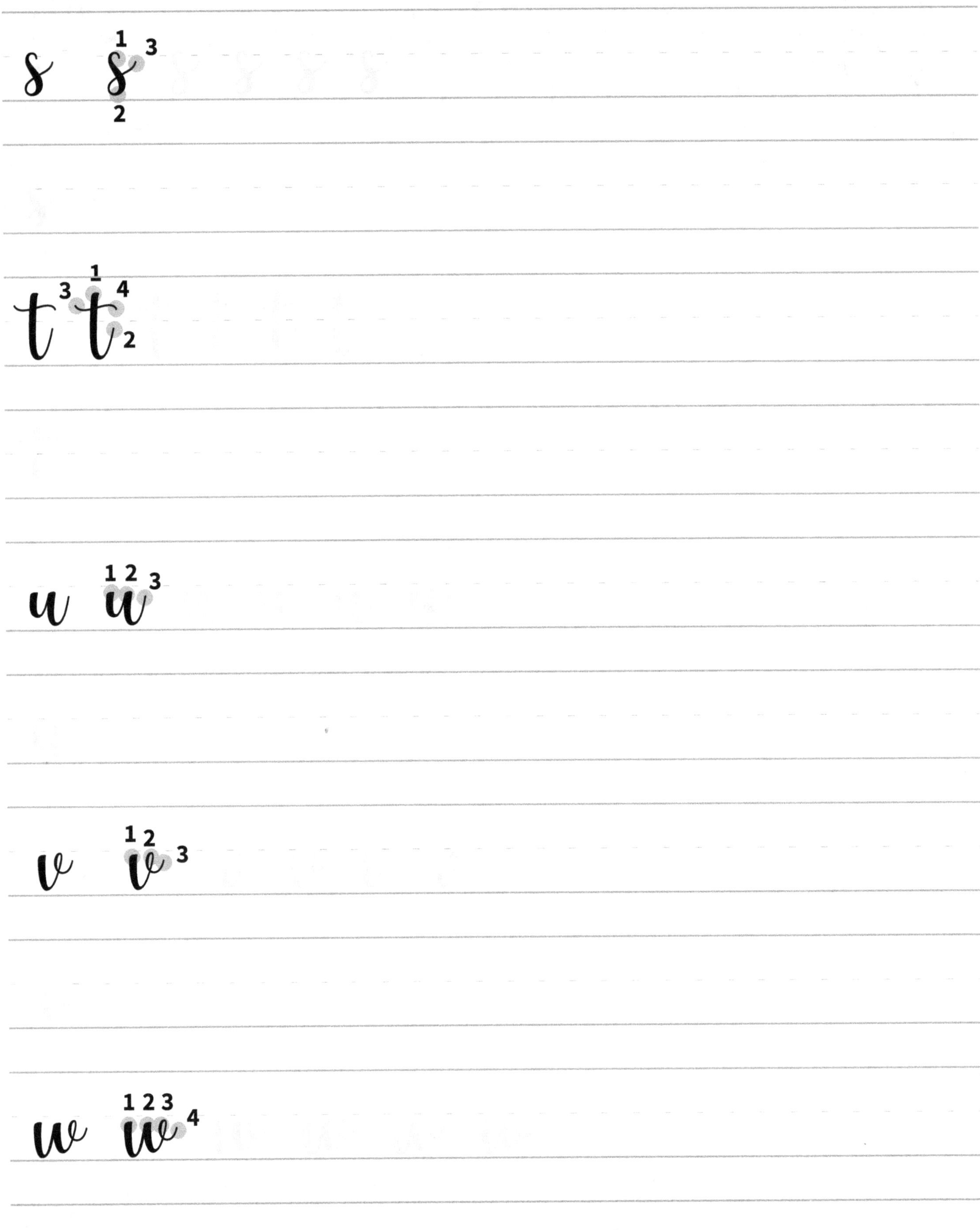

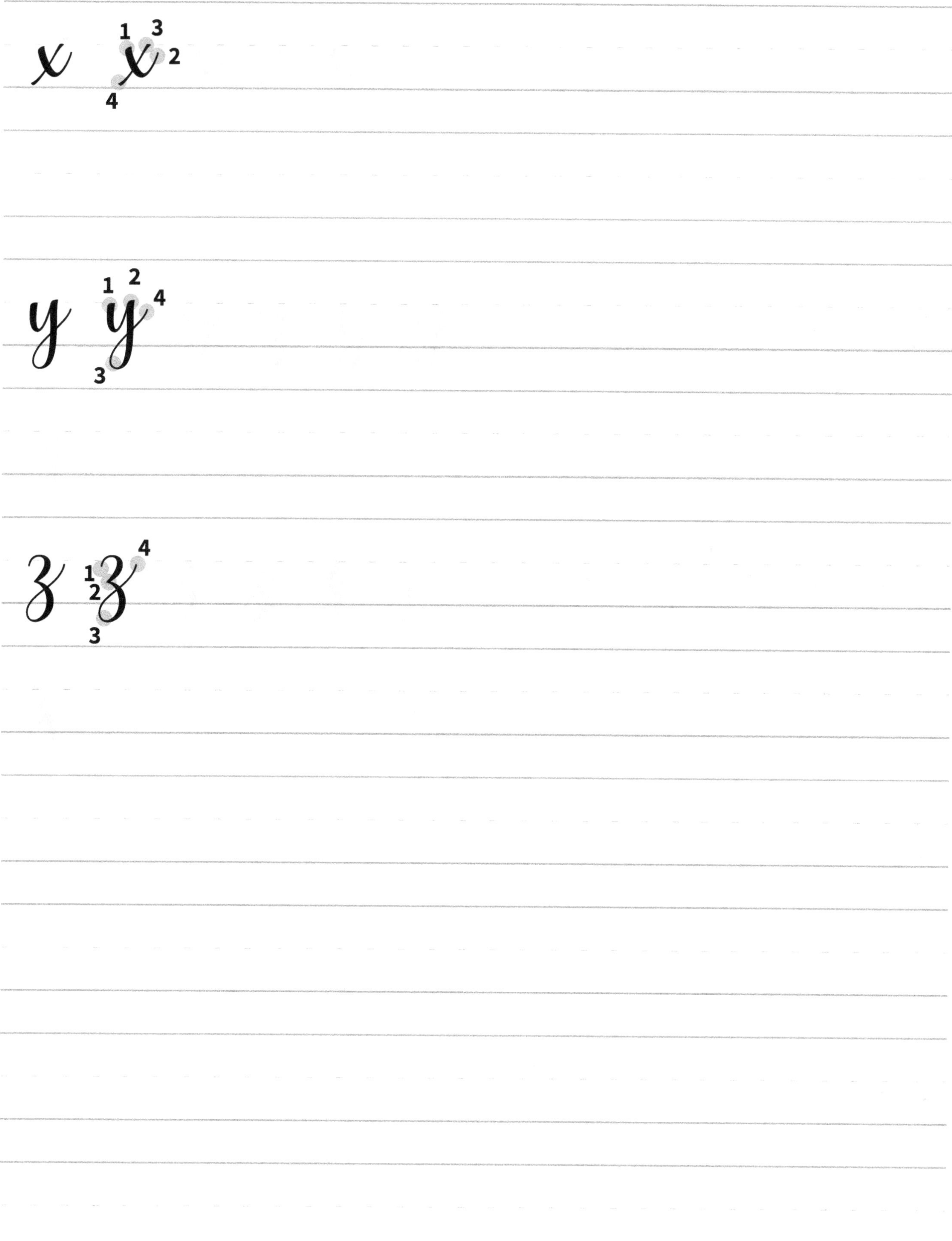

Words

writing

ROSE

life

CAT

zebra

WALK

season

GIRL

journal

Phrases

PRACTICE WRITING THE FOLLOWING PHRASES.

Work smart, not hard.

Be the best version of you.

You have what it takes.

One day at a time.

Style 2

Letters

PRACTICE WRITING THE UPPERCASE AND LOWERCASE LETTERS.

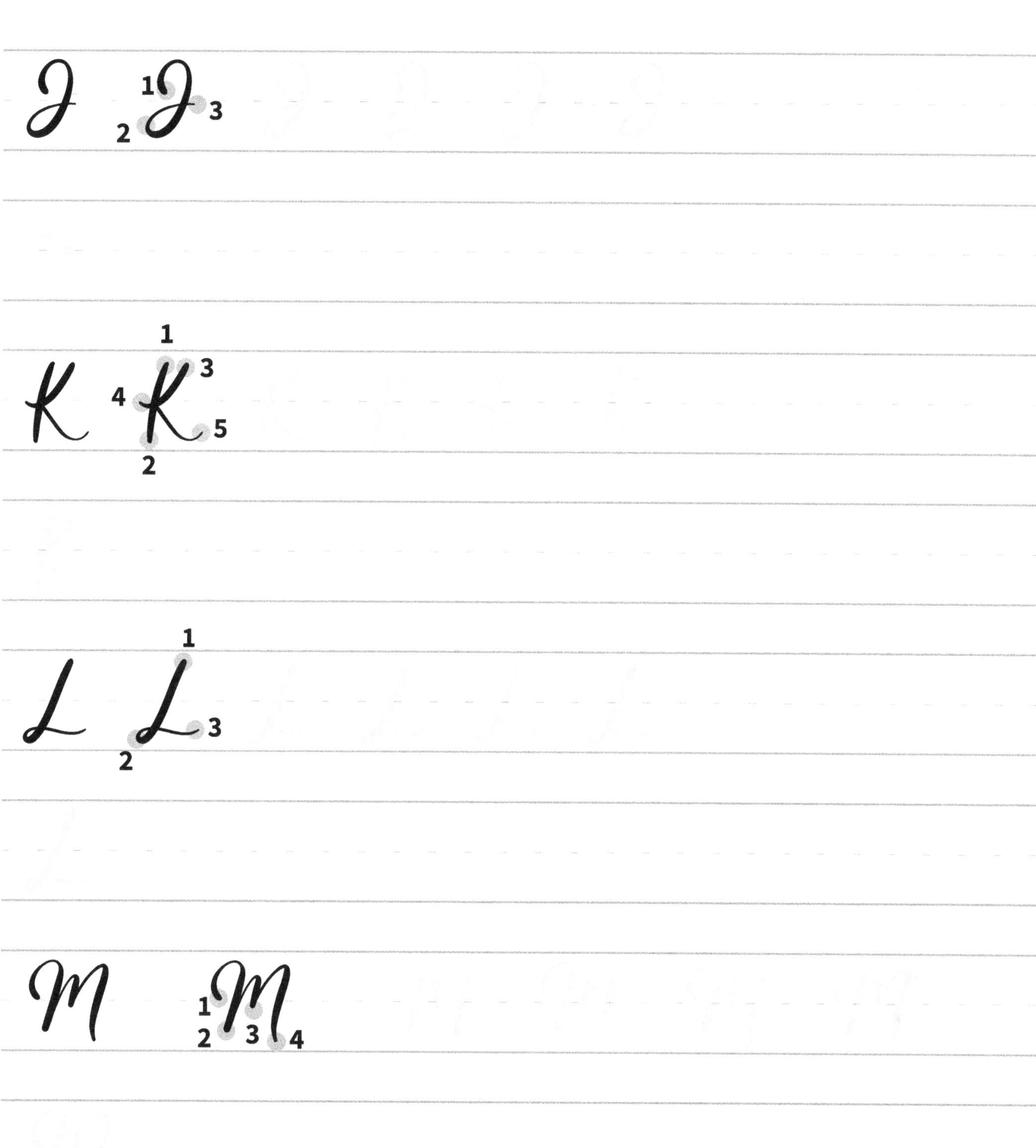

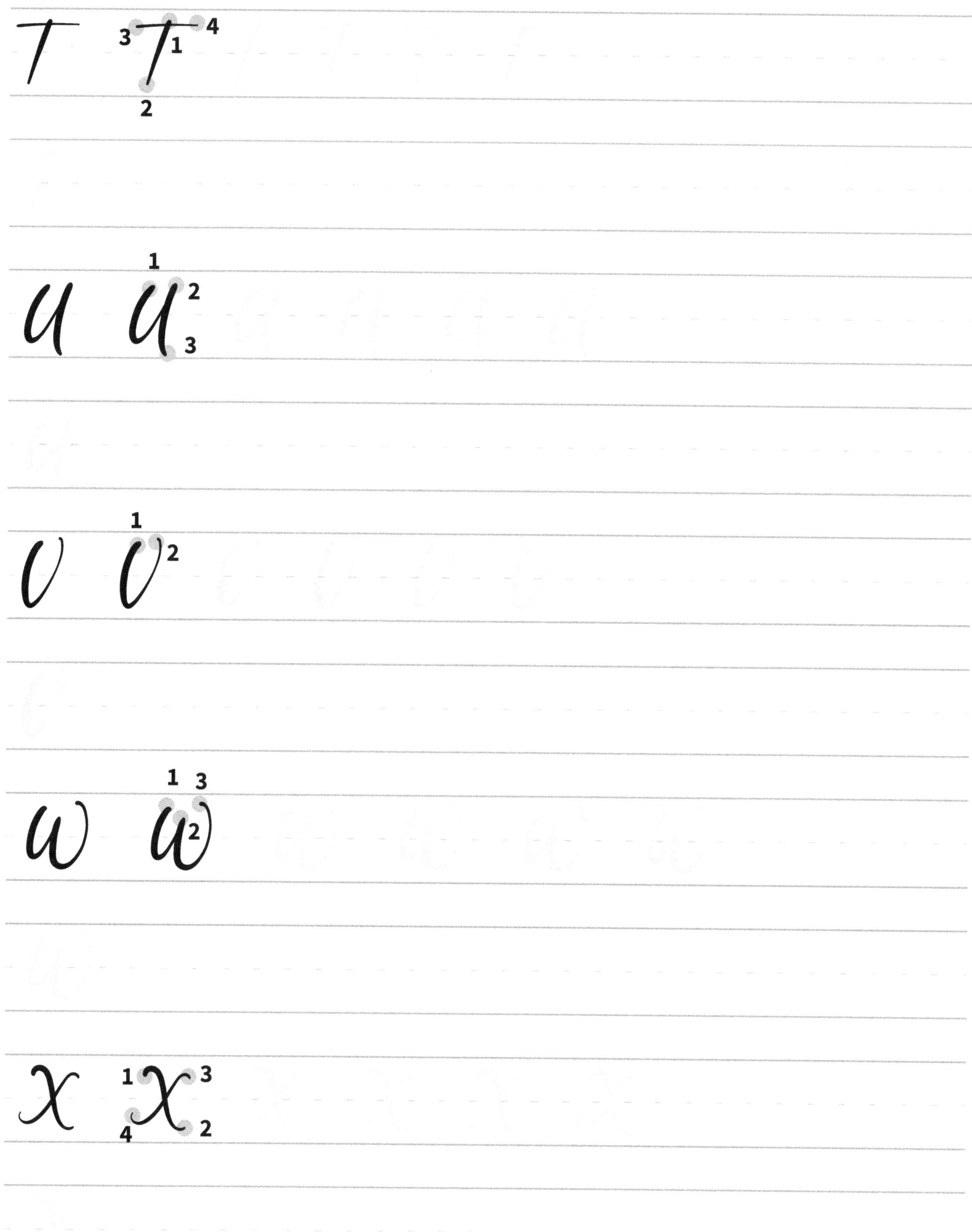

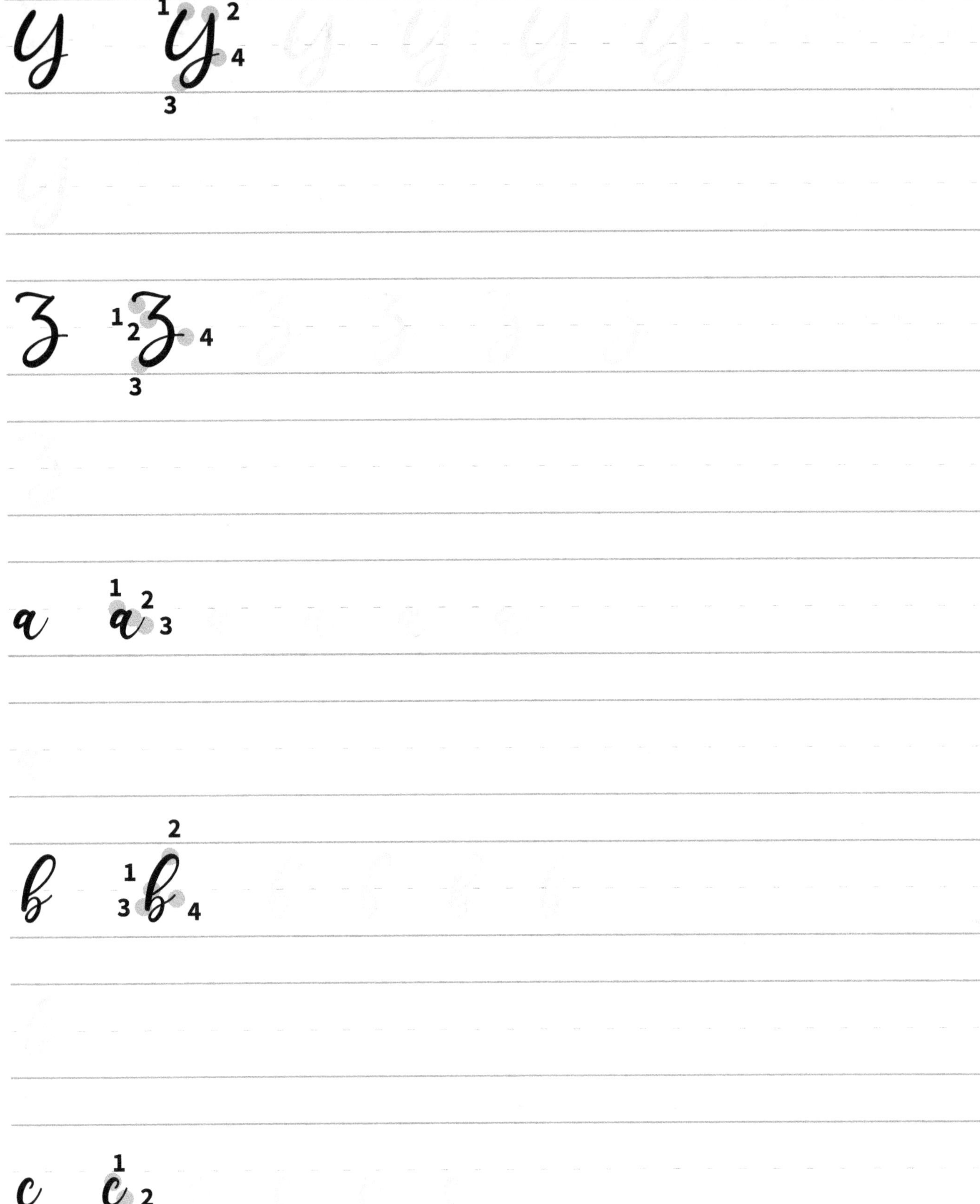

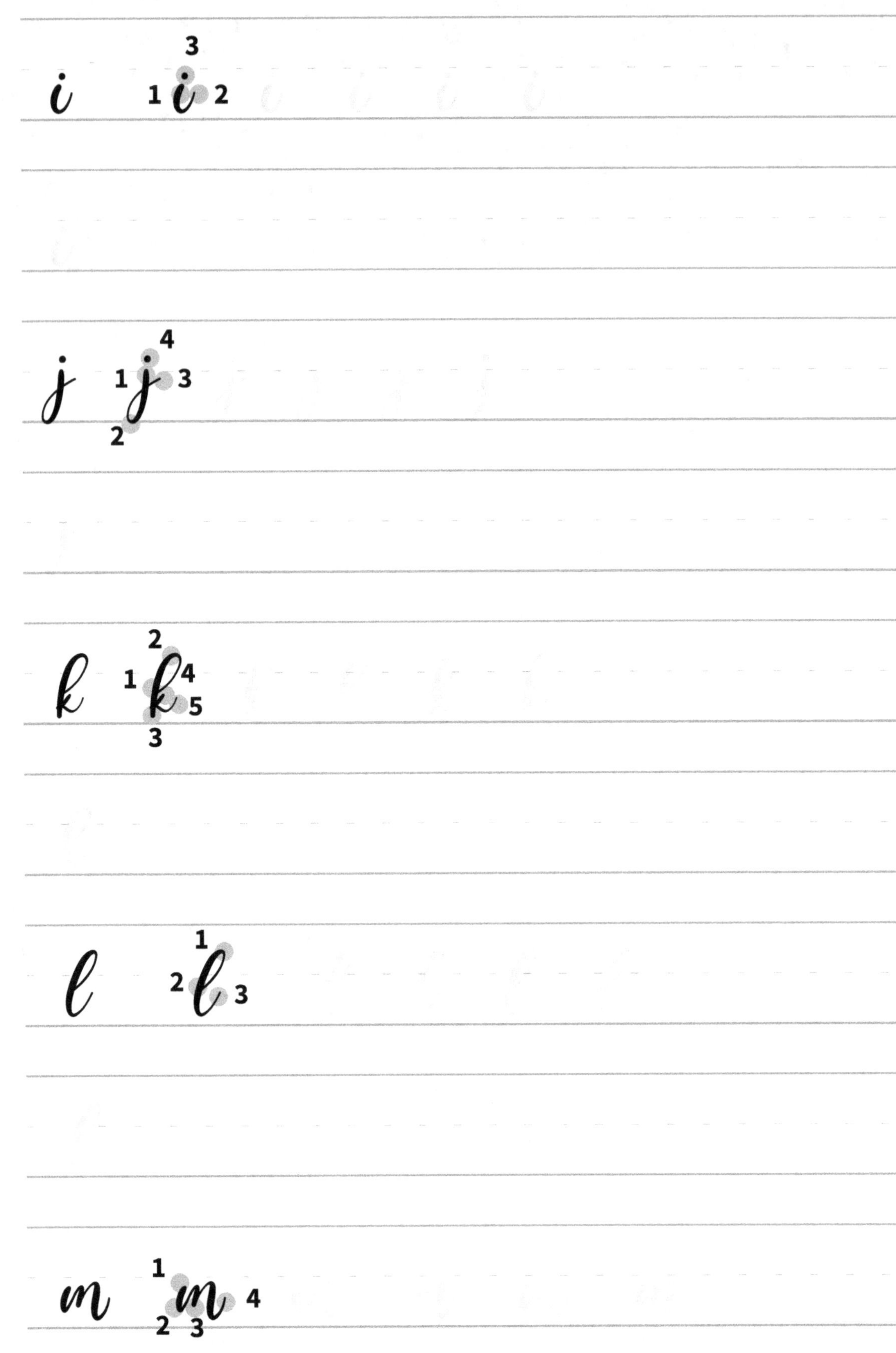

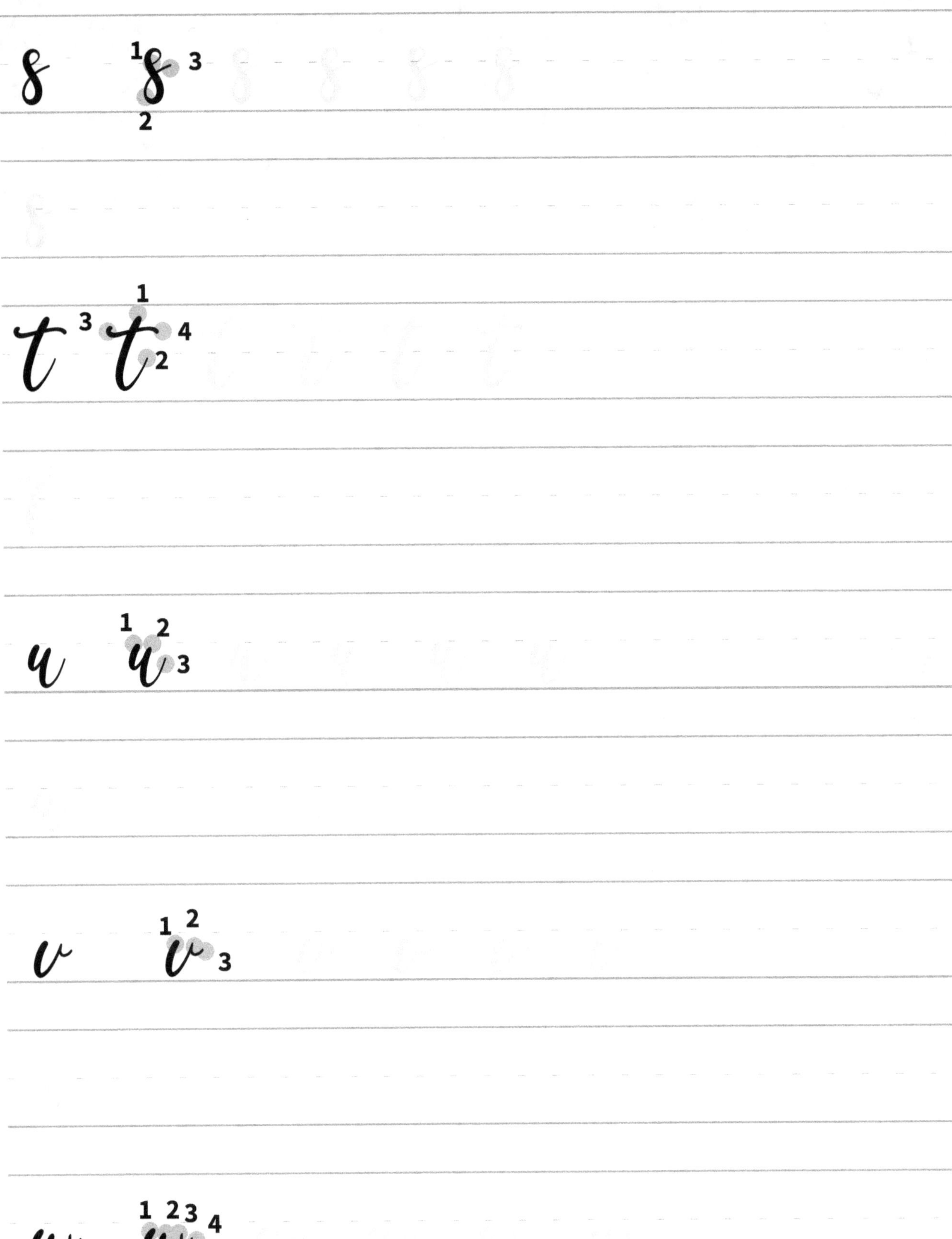

Words

reading

HALF

beauty

LOVE

awesome

DOG

drink

WINE

notebook

Phrases

PRACTICE WRITING THE FOLLOWING PHRASES.

Remember why you started.

You are strong.

Take care of yourself.

Life has its ups and downs.

Style 3

Letters

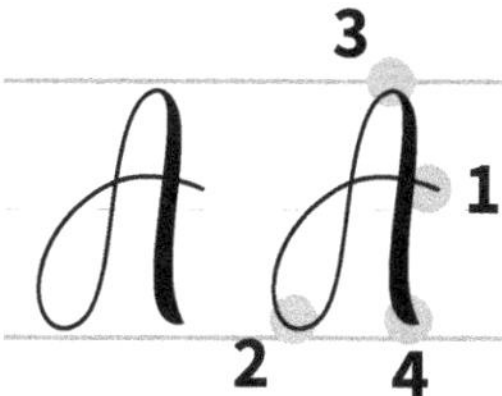

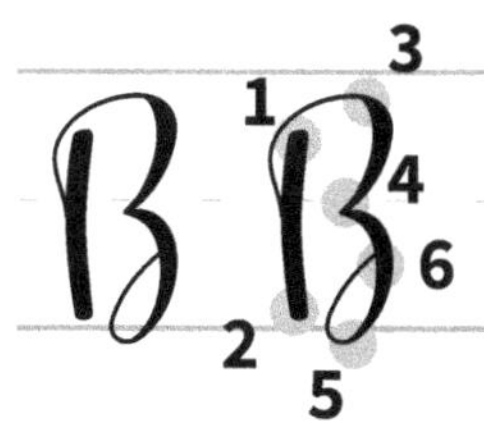

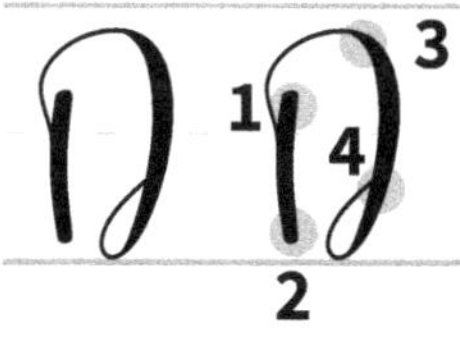

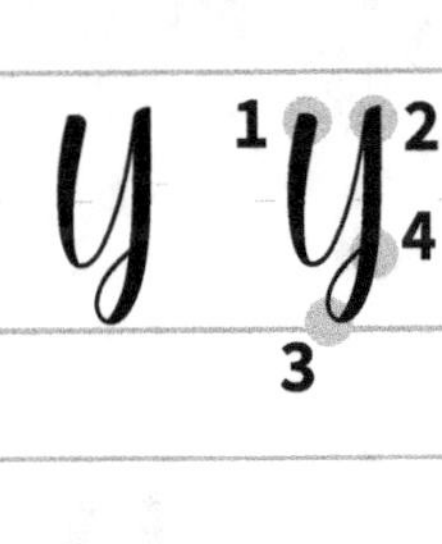

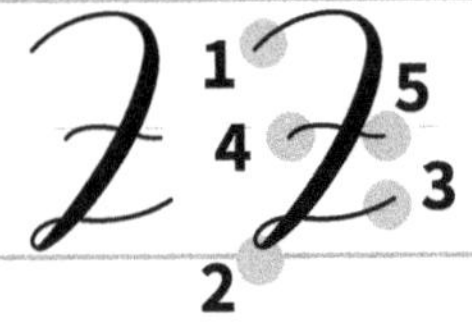

sweet

JAR

weather

COLD

people

WARM

desire

BABY

happiness

Phrases

PRACTICE WRITING THE FOLLOWING PHRASES.

Stay hustling.

Every day is a second chance.

Believe in yourself.

Do less with more focus.

Style 4

Letters

PRACTICE WRITING THE UPPERCASE AND LOWERCASE LETTERS.

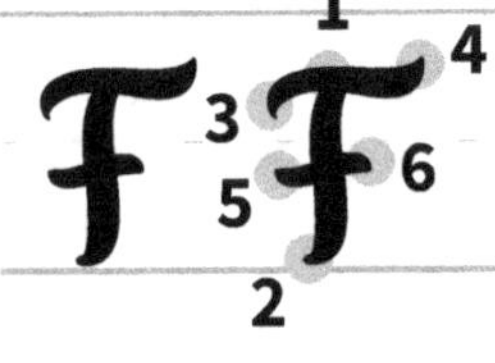

J $\quad$ J

K $\quad$ K

L $\quad$ L

M $\quad$ M

N $\quad$ N

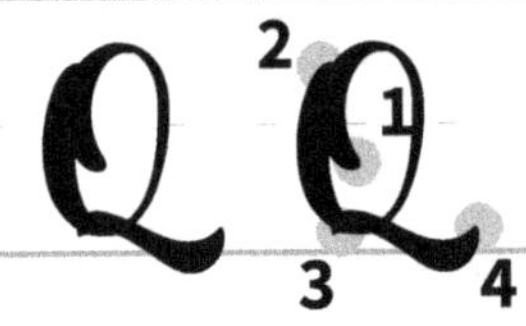

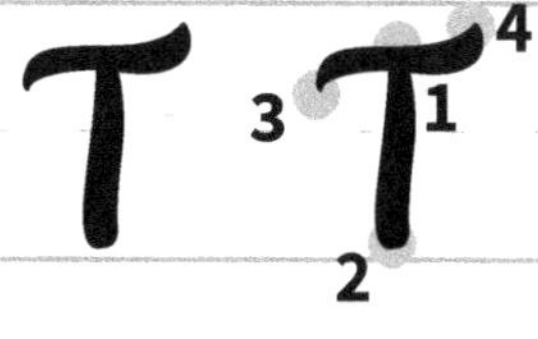

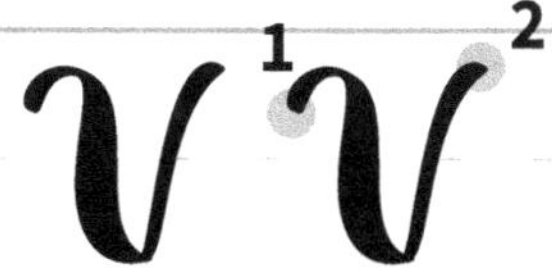

y ^{1}y^2
  $_3$

z ^{1}z^2
  $_3$ $_4$

a ^{1}a^2$_3$

b ^{1}b^3
  $_2$ $_4$

c c^1$_2$

d   d

e   e

f f

g g

h h

n $\overset{1}{\underset{2}{n}}$ 3

o $\overset{1}{\underset{2}{o}}$

p $\overset{1}{\underset{4}{\underset{2}{p}}}$ 3

q $\overset{1}{\underset{2}{q}}$ 3 4

r $\overset{2}{\underset{1}{r}}$ 3

s

t

u

v

w

Words

PRACTICE WRITING THE FOLLOWING WORDS.

interest

CALM

passion

GOOD

hunger

MISS

learning

RACE

growth

Phrases

PRACTICE WRITING THE FOLLOWING PHRASES.

Keep going.

You got this.

Choose joy.

Smile often.

Style 5

Letters

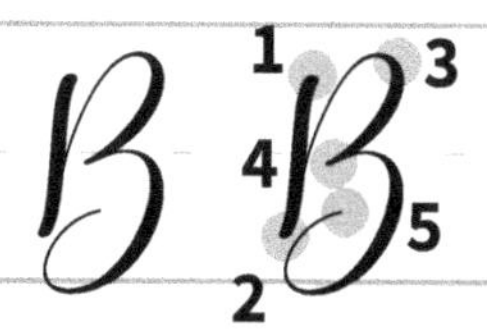

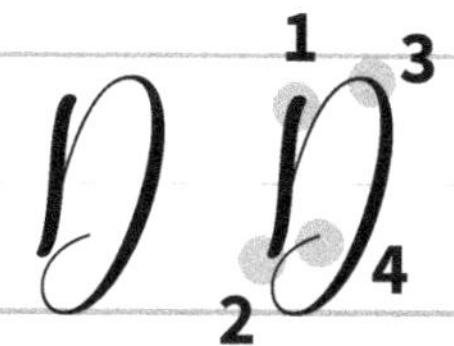

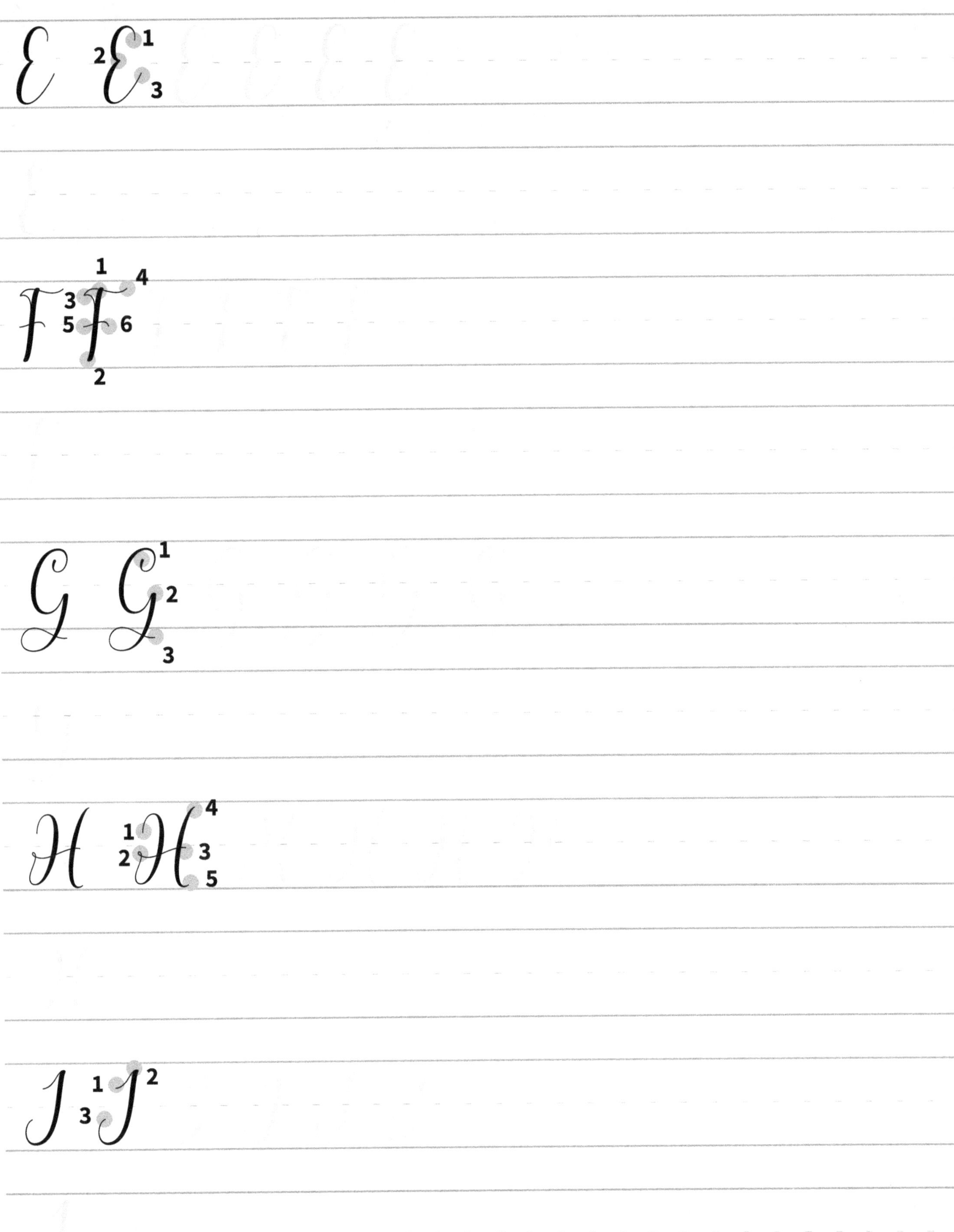

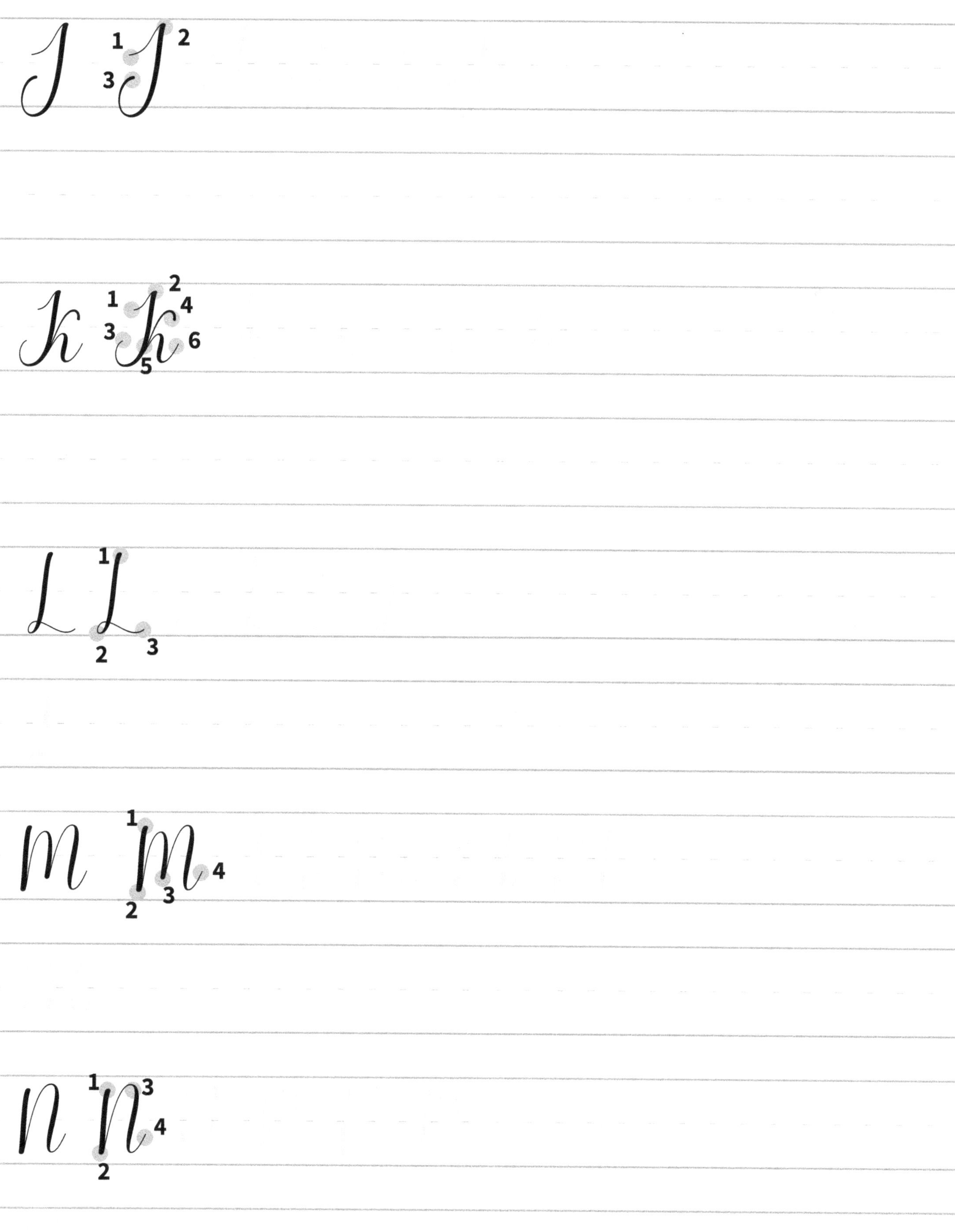

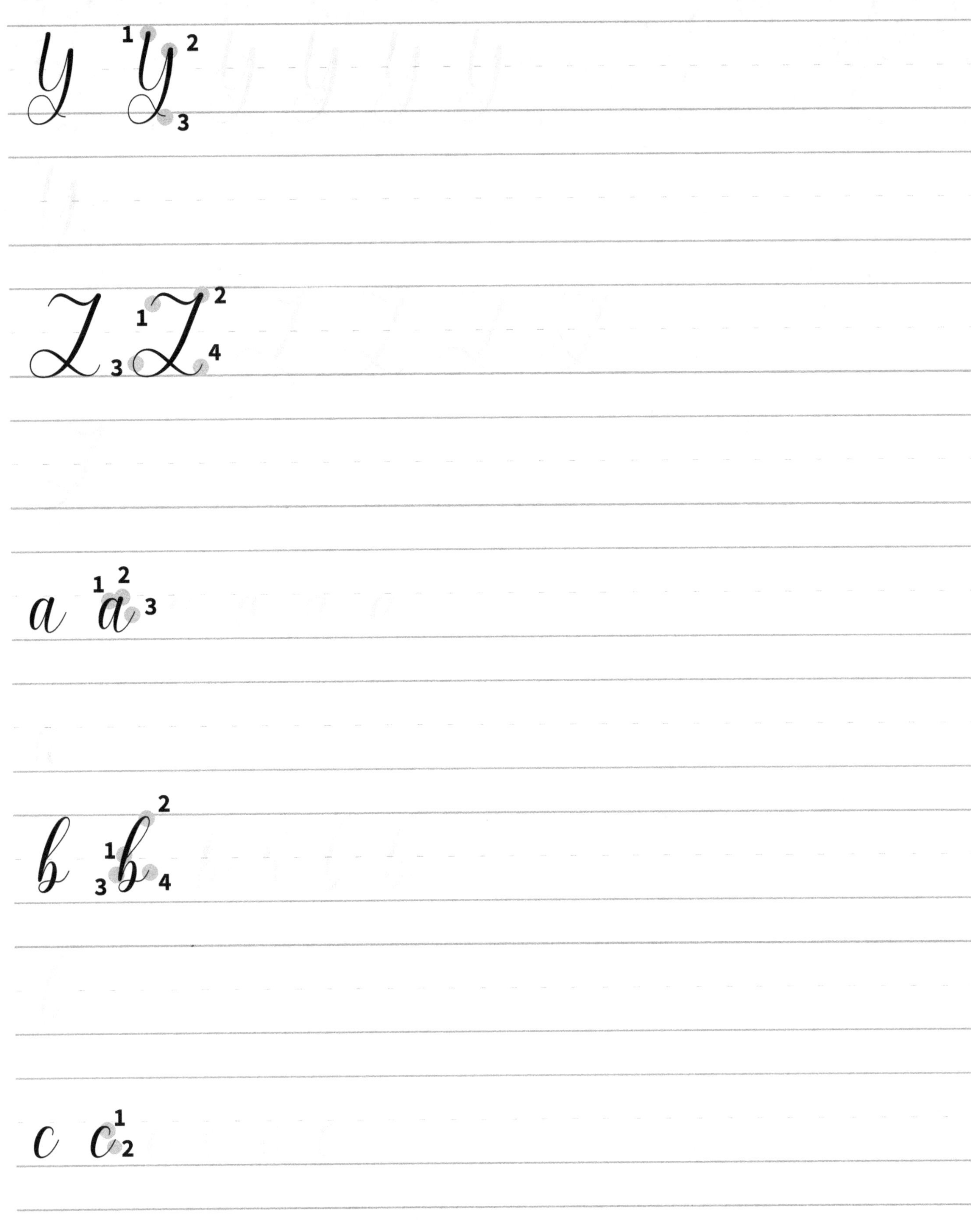

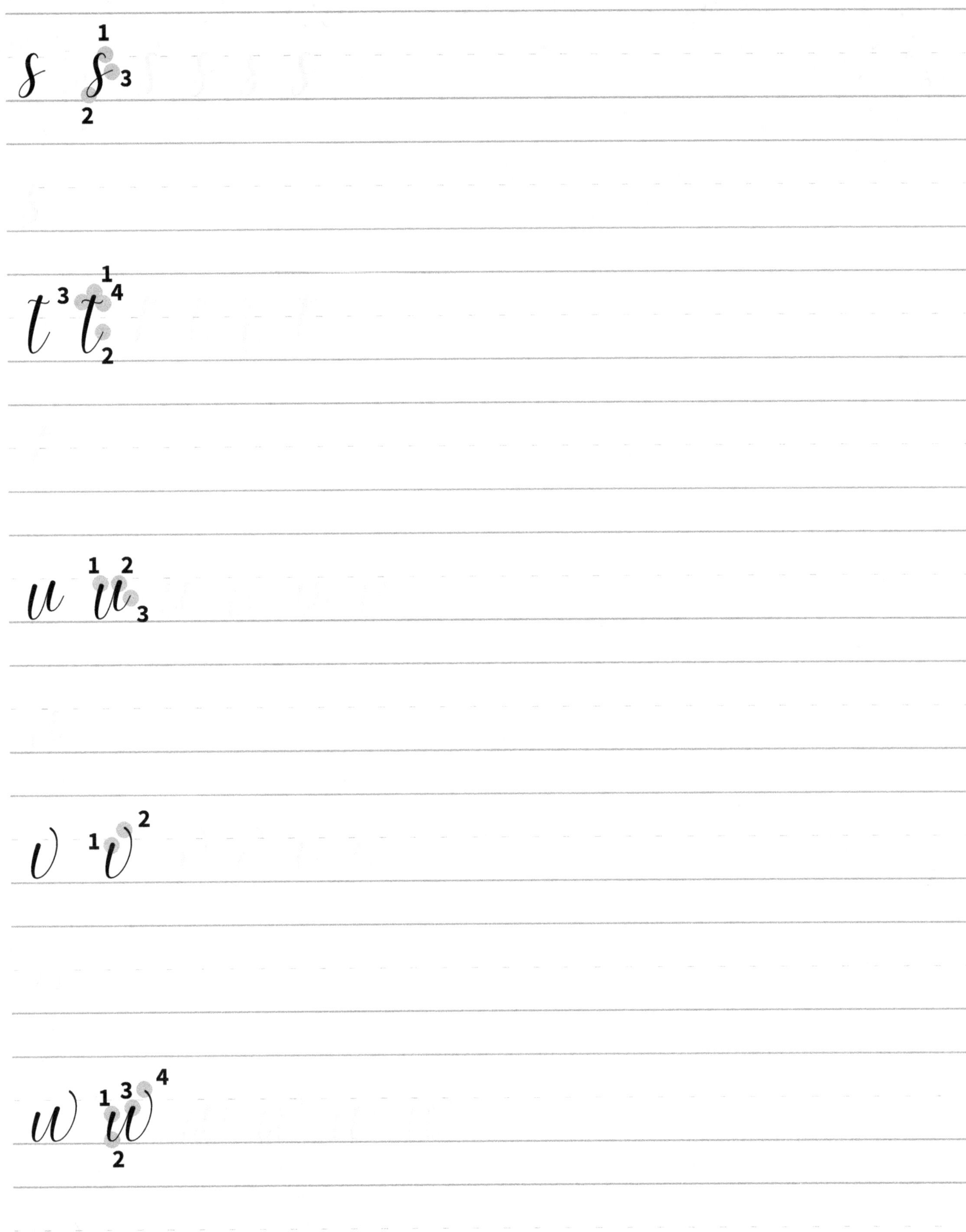

Words

month

BLUE

motivation

GAME

awareness

ZONE

habit

SOFT

elephant

Phrases

Be a game-changer.

Learn to rest not to quit.

Progress, not perfection.

Your limit is only you.

Style 6

Letters

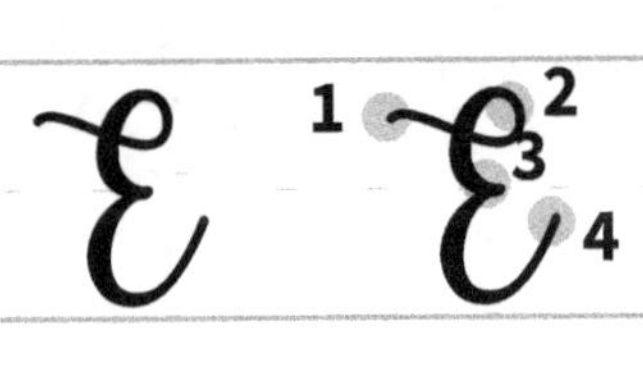

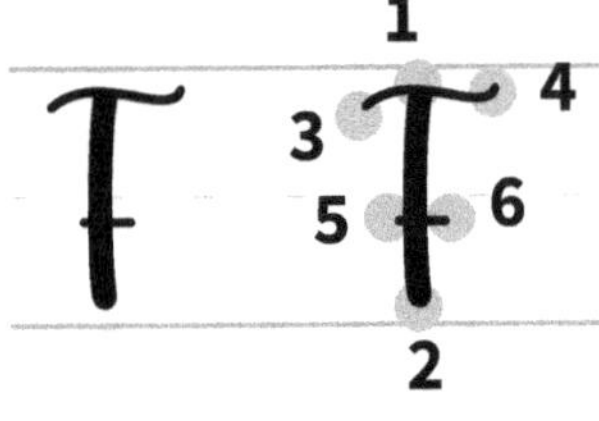

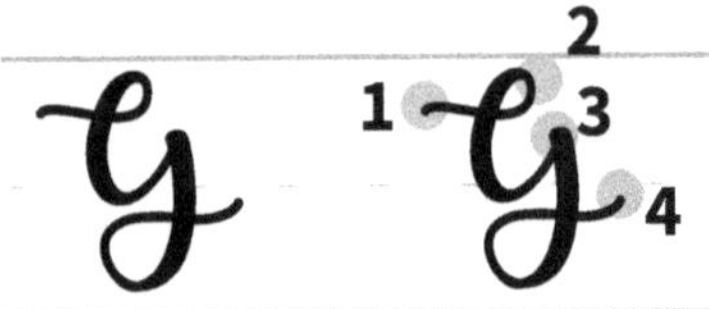

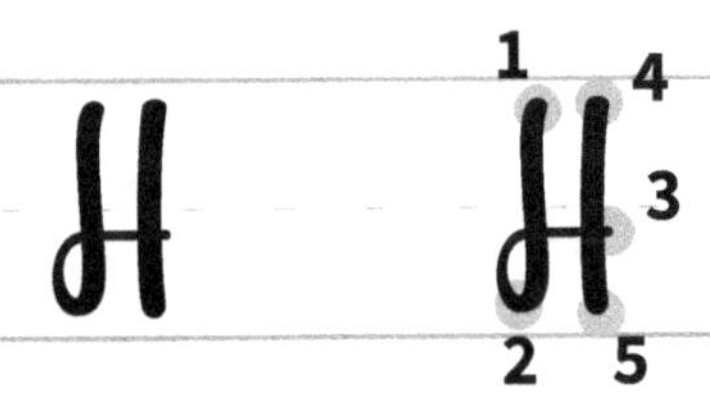

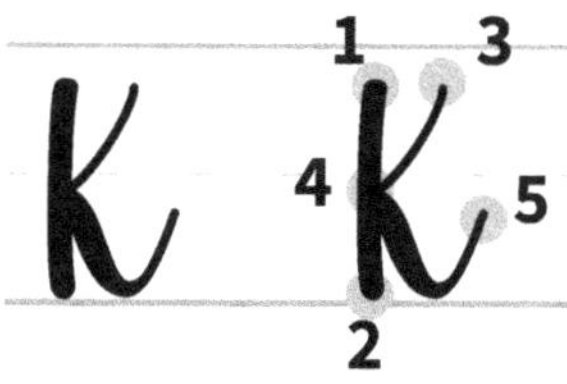

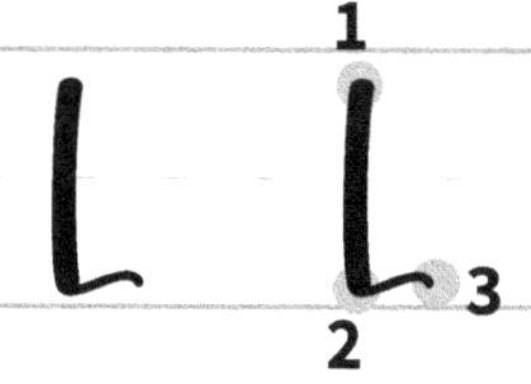

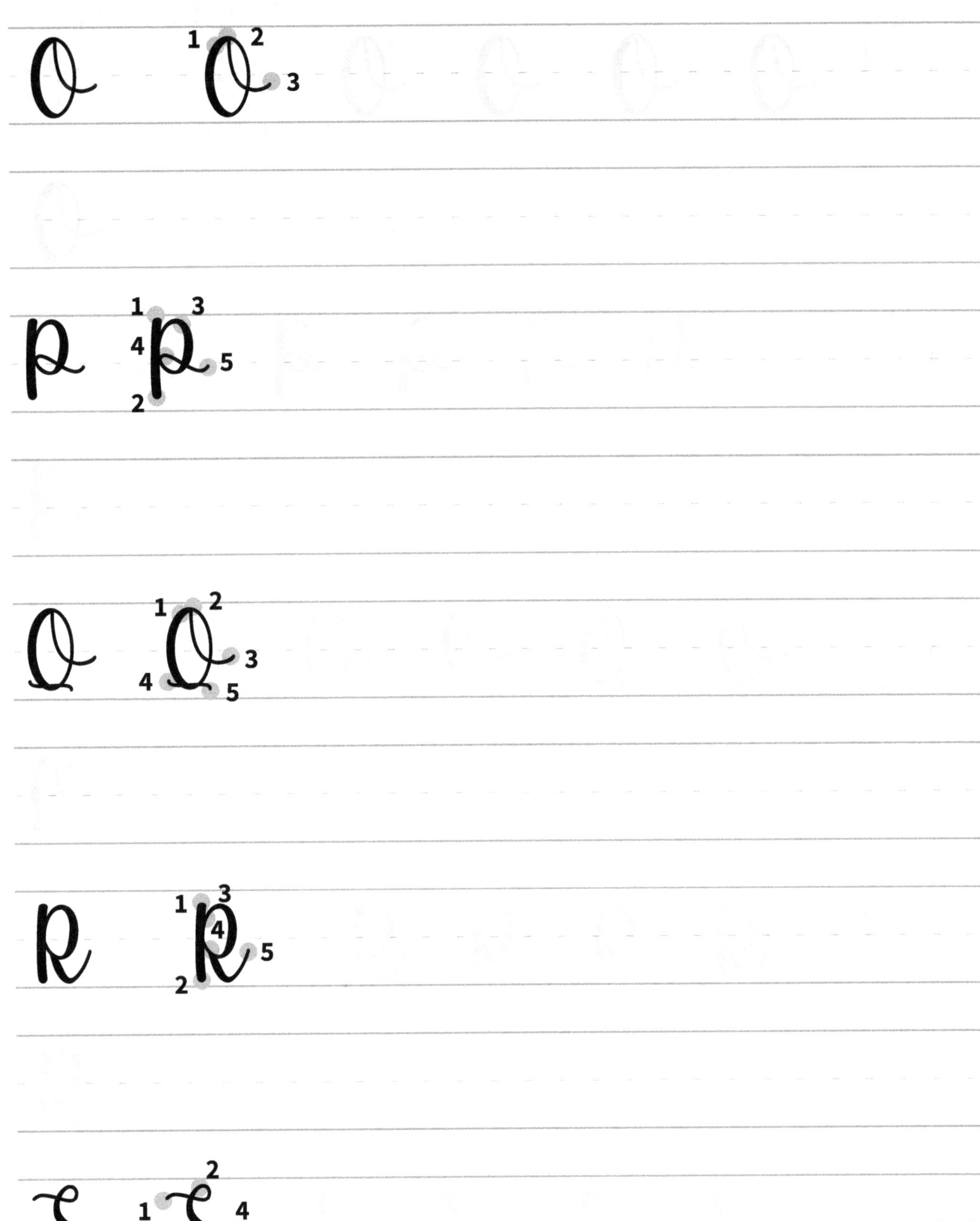

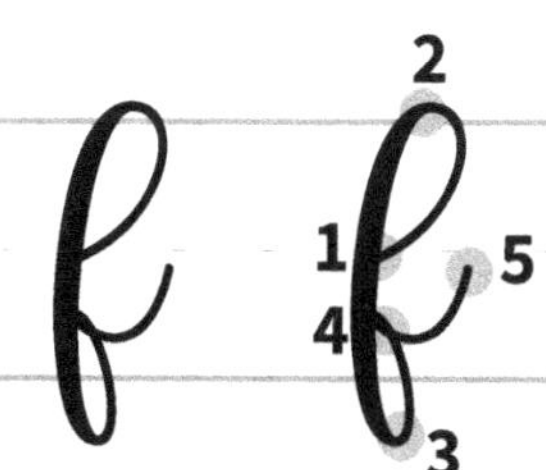

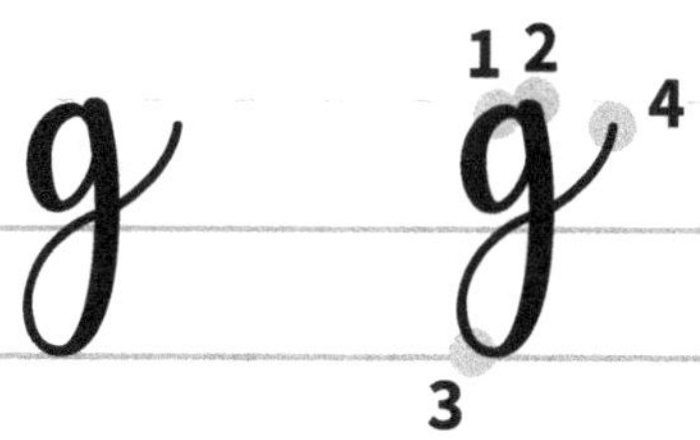

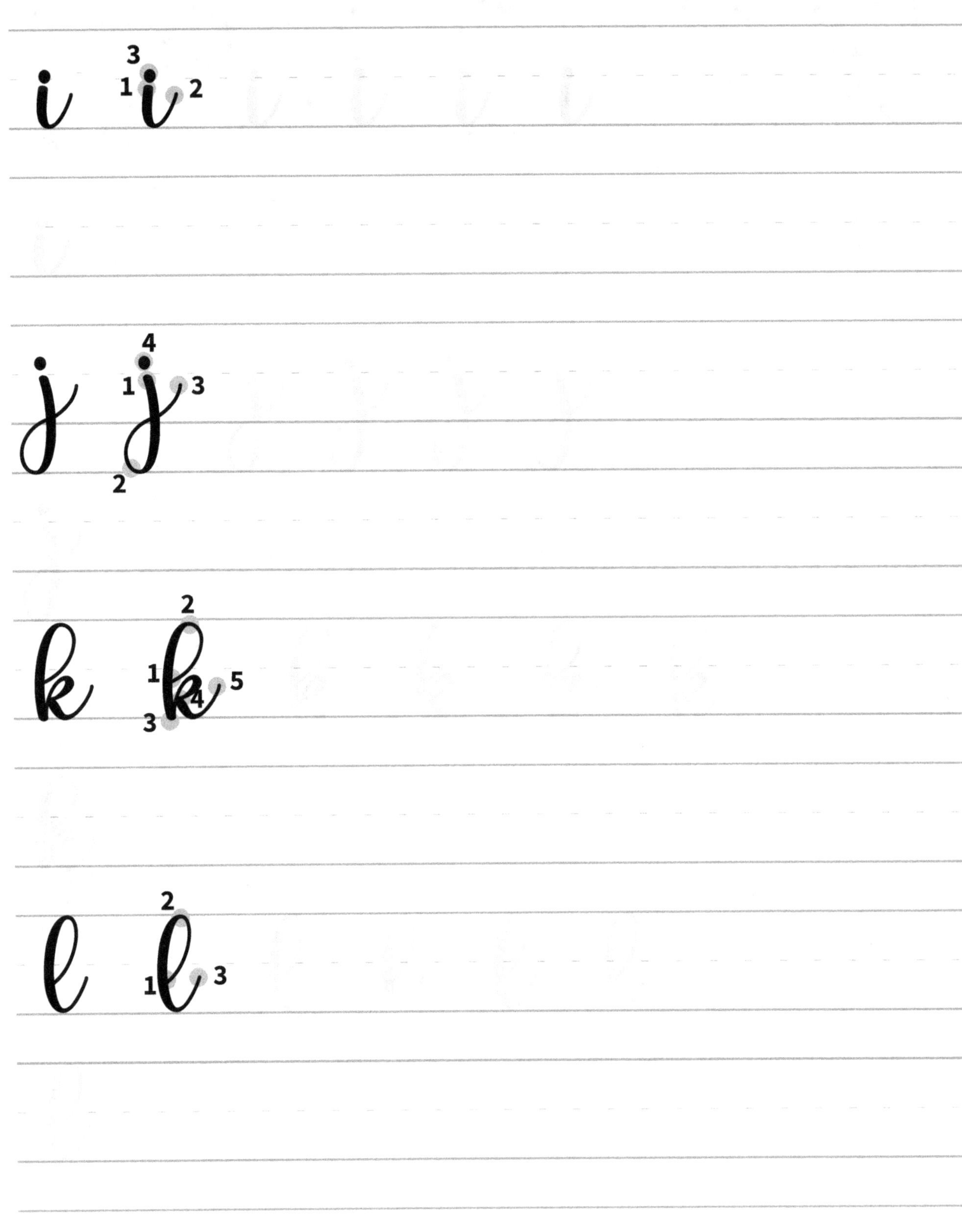

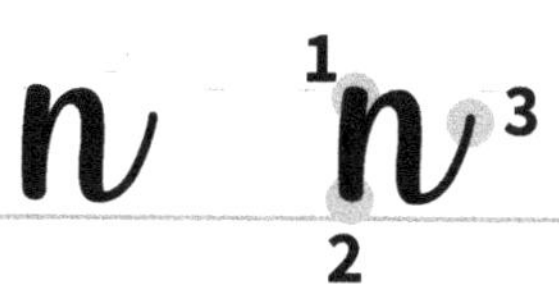

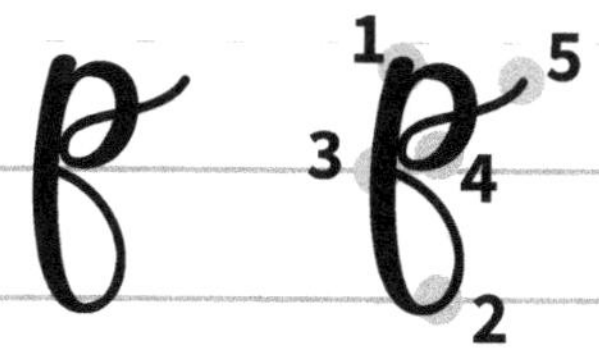

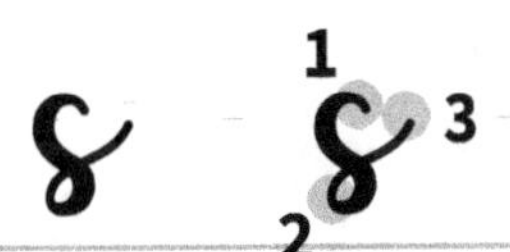

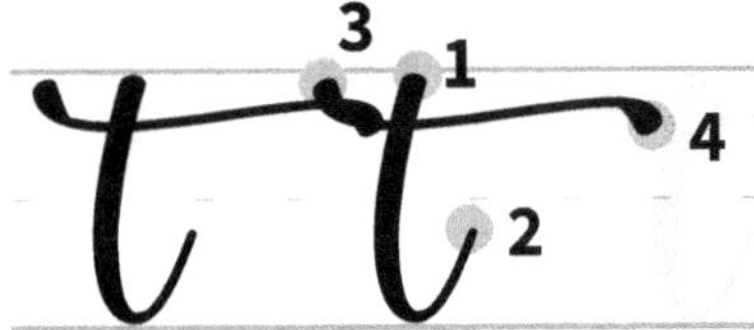

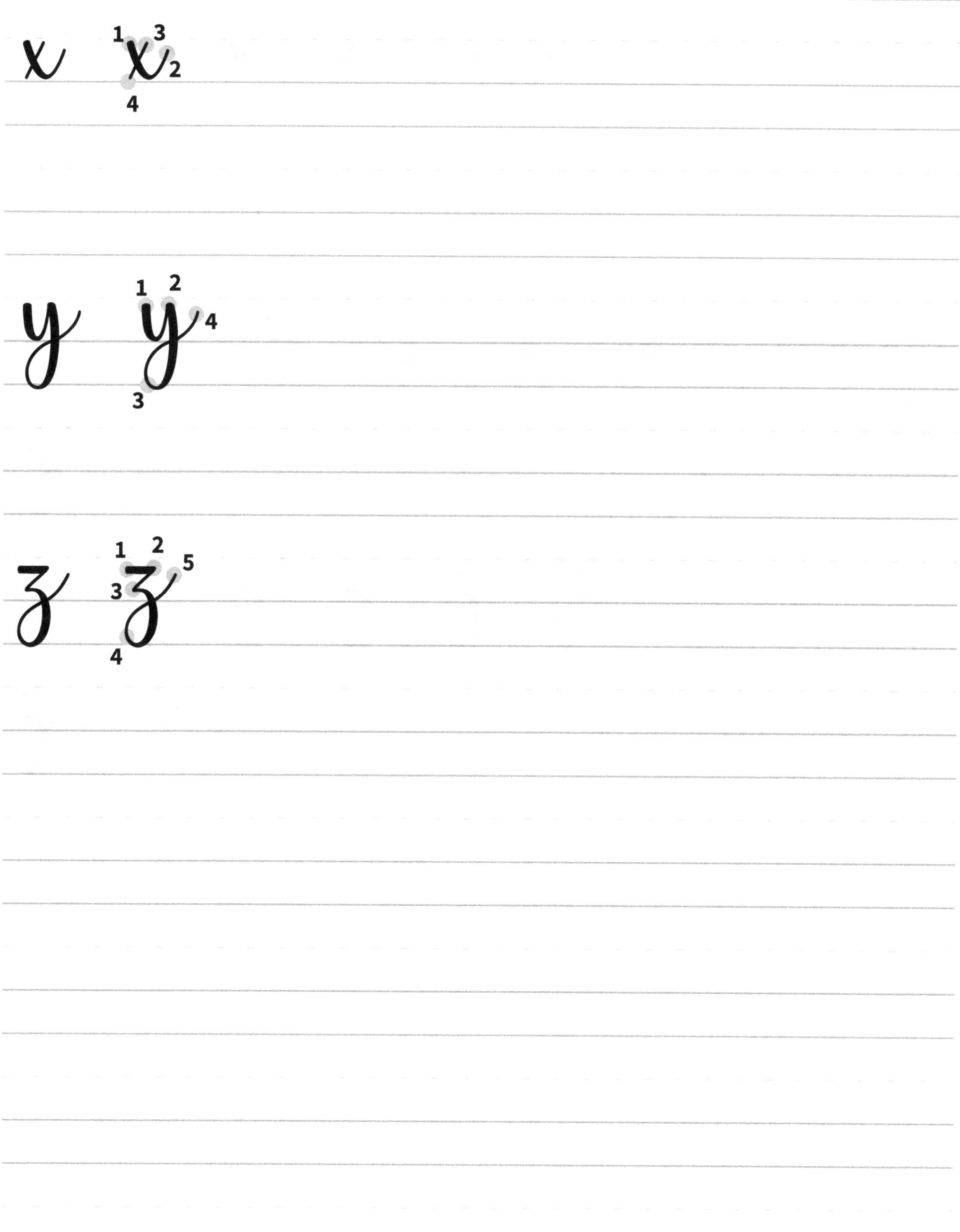

Words

monkey

SHIP

cloud

YEAR

fitness firness

PAST

water

MAIL

laptop

Phrases

You are amazing.

Celebrate every win.

You are enough.

Don't quit.

Hand Lettering Practice

MADE
with
love

Let's
go
travel

a very
Happy
BIRTHDAY
to you

IT'S THE
Little
THINGS
IN LIFE

TRUE
Love
LASTS
Forever

KEEP
Calm
&
LOVE

TALK
Less
— DO —
More

Failure
IS Success ON
PROGRESS

Someone must keep on FIGHTING until our life time is OVER

IF YOU
never try
you will
NEVER
KNOW

Thank you for your purchase and we hope you enjoyed our book!

Your feedback on Amazon is greatly appreciated as
it lets us know how we are doing!

For all inquiries, email us at
rosetrifoliapress@gmail.com